89-689

DEMCO

Book
of
Country

Volume II

Don & Carol Raycraft

Book
of
Country

Volume II

Don and Carol Raycraft

Collector Books
A Division of Schroeder Publishing Co., Inc.

The current values in this book should be used only as a guide. They are not intended to set prices, which vary from one section of the country to another. Auction prices as well as dealer prices vary greatly and are affected by condition as well as demand. Neither the Author nor the Publisher assumes responsibility for any losses that might be incurred as a result of consulting this guide.

Acknowledgments

Tom Heintz and Israel Shapiro
Joe and Opal Pickens
Lynn Mladineo
Vernon Pottery, Virginia Beach, Virginia
Jerry Beaumont
Chet Chylinski
Barb and Dale Weingart
Carla and Steve Katzberger
Ann and Tom Hixson
Norma Jordan
Lee and Cindy Sawyer
Jo Ann Garrett
Cory Roop
Alex Hood
Steve Rhodes
Rose Holtzclaw
Ellen Tatem
Jan Farley
Karen Shields & Sharon Bauer
Al and Barb Blumberg
Bon Aqua, Tennessee Pottery
Jack Hughes
Mary Myers
Ken and Carllene Elliott
Delores Teeters - Country Gingham
Bernie Green
Ron and Ann Roop
1818 House Antiques - Lancaster, Kentucky
Ken and Diane Strong

Photography

Carol Raycraft
R. Craig Raycraft
Charles Dull
Sid and Eileen Vernon
Tom and Ann Hixson
Lynn Mladineo
Jo Ann Garrett
Chet Chylinski
Jan Farley

Introduction

We began to collect American country antiques in the mid-1960's. At that point we lived in a small central Illinois community that contained a bank, restaurant, one stop light, grocery store, barber shop, and "variety" store. In the Midwest a "variety" store typically sells everything from shoe laces to shingles. This particular store was especially interesting because it was operated by two sisters who arrived every day at 8 a.m., closed for an hour at noon and went home each evening promptly at 5:30. Seldom was their daty interrupted by customers. They carried the day's limited receipts in a galvanized bucket and lived in a house with grass that hadn't been cut since Herbert Hoover was in the White House. The store had been established by the sisters' father who had died in the early 1950's. From that point until the death of the sisters, it was business as usual every day with merchandise packed from floor to ceiling.

Several people had tried over the years to purchase the Diamond Dye cabinets and the cast iron coffee grinder on the counter, but the sisters would not sell store fixtures as antiques. They only sold the merchandise on the shelves. We did not realize it at the time, but the merchandise was made up primarily of antiques. There ware cast iron string holders, feather Christmas trees and German ornaments, toys, wooden butter paddles, and a huge variety of food, soap, and tobacco containers with colorful labels and contents that would turn public health officials purple.

The stock did not change very much beacuse local people seldom were patrons. They had grown up with the store, knew the sisters, but had no interest in what was inside. We ventured in periodically to look around and buy a small item for two dollars. Neither the merchandise or the prices changed very much.

In retrospect we were foolish not to have filled a trunk with as much as we could afford to buy, but we appreciate now the opportunity we had and have learned from the experience. We were not aware at the time of any books or price guides that would have instructed us or knew of any individuals with enough knowledge to assist us.

Eventually we began to figure out what we liked and where to go to find it. We decided we wanted to collect the simple pine furniture that decorated rural American homes during the 1830-1870 period. Most antiques shops, we discovered, were primarily operated by elderly women who filled their businesses with oak china cabinets, colored glass, dolls, paper weights, and postcards. The "primitives" were always piled in an attached garage or down some steep steps in a wet basement with five-foot ceilings.

As most collectors find out, it is a major accomplishment to finally determine what you can't live without. In the late 1960's we were on a first name basis with many of the antiques dealers in Illinois, northern Indiana, and western Ohio. We learned to appreciate a piece of furniture for what it was. If it had been recently painted, stripped, or reworked, we were not interested in purchasing it. With a station wagon and $300.00 it was not impossible to find a dry sink, a "bird" jug, a pie safe, two nights in a Holiday Inn, and the opportunity to eat at the Golden Lamb Inn in Lebanon, Ohio. We made a significant number of trips and learned from each venture.

At that point, most of the people who purchased

blanket chests and cupboards wanted to "see the wood." Very few people paid any attention to a painted finish. Paint was something that was removed as quickly and as effortlessly as possible. Even then we did not see a significant number of sinks or chests with their original paint. When we go to shows today, we see considerably more painted furniture than we did twenty years ago. A close inspeciton of much of this furniture suggests that the piece is usually much older than its paint.

There are many factors that affect the value or desirability of American country antiques. A signature impressed into the underside of a chair seat or a bowl made from burl rather than maple are critical. The specific shade of blue paint on a cupboard or desk can mean hundreds or thousands of dollars in evaluating it. Blue, bittersweet, yellow, green, and red are popular colors. White, brown, or black do not help the value and are much less in demand. If two exact cupboards are placed next to each other and one is refinished and the other carries its original bright blue paint, the difference in price should be staggering. The refinished cupboard could be worth $1200.00 and the painted cupboard, its structural twin, may be priced at $3500.00. The only difference between the cupboards is the $2300.00 coat of blue paint.

Over the past 20 years, we have written more than 30 books about American antiques. The topics have ranged from furniture, Shaker, and baskets to stoneware and country store collectibles. In this second *Book of Country*, we want to provide you with some of the insights we have picked up over the years.

The photographs that are used to illustrate this book have been carefully selected. As has been the case with all of our books, the emphasis is on items that you as a collector can still find. It may cost you more than you want to pay, and you may have to go farther than you want to travel, but it is still out there waiting.

It serves no purpose to discuss Pilgrim Century furniture and great 18th century pewter cupboards because most of us will probably never have the resources or the opportunity to own an example. Wallace Nutting has already done the job much better than we could ever hope to do, and he did it 60 years ago.

Right:
Refinished step-back cupboard, c. mid 19th century.

Bottom:
Pine table, "scrubbed top," c. 1850.

Left:
Refinished corner cupboard, found in Kentucky, c. 1830's, paneled doors.

Bottom:
Pine blanket chest, unusual paneled sides, original painted finish, c. 1840's.

Top:
Dome top pine chest with elaborately painted finish. Examples of country furniture like this chest are extremely difficult to date because the paint is not nearly as old as the piece. When 19th century furniture is "antiqued" at some point in the 20th century, it makes it awkward. A piece like this could fool someone into writing a large check.

Right:
Pine "jelly" or storage cupboard, Kentucky, c. 1870, exceptional painted finish.

Left:

Child's ladder-back arm chair with splint seat, c. 1880's. This chair has probably lost several inches off its legs over the years because the stretchers are much too close to the floor. The stretchers (rungs) are correctly worn and the chair is "right." Occasionally chairs that have lost height are "pieced out" with 2" to 4" added to each leg and the paint matched to cover the alterations.

Right:

Hepplewhite two-drawer blanket chest, high bracket base, original brasses, refinished, New England, c. 1830. Bowback Windsor chair, c. 1840, dark green paint, New England.

Top:
Refinished trestle table, 19th century. When we first saw this table for sale 20 years ago, it was priced at $750.00. At that point, $750.00 was a lot of money, but it was the best piece of "country" furniture we had ever seen. It had "bread board ends" and appeared to be in its original condition. The problem with the table is the word "country." Twenty years of looking for other tables and visits to shops around the nation have convinced us that many pieces of furniture found in New England and the middle west probably began life in Mexico and Spain and not in the United States. This table is a classic example of such a piece.

Right:
Refinished 24-drawer storage chest with new porcelain knobs, c. early 1900's. Green scrubbed top side table, pine, c. 1880.

Left:
24-drawer storage chest, refinished, c. late 19th century.

Right:
Pine cupboard, original painted finish, possibly Canadian in origin, c. 1860.

Top:
Apothecary chest with 20 numbered drawers and painted finish, mid-19th century.

Right:
"High country" Federal chest of drawers, c. 1820's, found in Kentucky.

Left:
Pine cupboard, painted finish of questionable age, possibly cut down at base due to structural problems, probably midwestern in origin, c. late 19th century. The color is certainly unusual and not commonly seen on 19th century furniture. There should also be a little more wear around the turn buttons that hold the four doors closed. This is the type of piece that you do not mortgage a child or farm to buy.

Right:
Slat-back rocking chair, splint seat, c. 1885, found in Kentucky.

Scrubbed green farm table with a warped pine top and painted base, c. 1900. One of the earliest rules that a collector should learn is not to buy somebody's problems. A table like this one that is flawed, a great crock with a serious crack, or a rare sugar bucket without a lid but with a hefty price tag normally are avoided like sun-drenched potato salad at the Fourth of July picnic.

Uncommon storage cupboard with tin insert in door panel, North Carolina, c. 1870's.

Left:
Half-spindle back rocking chair in blue-grey paint, splint seat, New York state, c. 1870's. The interest in Shaker antiques has created an emotional market for anything that faintly resembles one of their products. If a rocking chair has turned finials and simple lines, it's Shaker. It makes no difference that it was made in Bloomington, Illinois by somebody's grandfather, it's Shaker. Keep in mind that the Shakers were mass-producing rocking chairs in eight sizes from the 1870's until the early 1940's. Their chairs were machine made, assembled, and dipped in a vat for color. They show no tool marks or deviations of any kind. This rocking chair is a piece of country furniture and considerably more appealing, though less valuable, than a production Shaker rocking chair.

Right:
Factory-made bedside stand, pine, "as found" condition, c. 1880-early 1900's. This piece of "cottage" furniture was mass produced in a late 19th century factory that specialized in inexpensive home furnishings. Over the years, it has picked up several coats of paint. If you back up the truck to add this to your collection, run over it before you load it and use the remnants for kindling.

Left:
Writing-arm Windsor chair, early 19th century, New England.

Right:
Painted pine cupboard, worn green paint, Virginia, mid 19th century.

Pine pie cupboard, brown paint, c. 1870's.

Open cupboard, partially stripped, found in North Carolina, c. 1880.

Left:
Late 19th century "barrel front" cupboard, stained exterior and painted interior.

Right:
Painted pine storage cupboard, c. 1870.

Unusual Kentucky sugar chest in blue paint with additional decoration and initials, c. 1840's.

Left:
Painted pine storage cupboard, blue paint with traces of white, c. 1875. In the home furnishing magazines that emphasize the "country look," we see many pieces of "painted" furniture that have only a miniscule portion of the original finish intact and belong on a back porch rather than in a living room. This is an excellent cupboard that has been scraped down to its original coat of blue paint. The white paint that remains creates a problem for us. The cupboard is functional and structurally sound but needs additional work to remove the remnants of white paint.

Right:
Unusual pine cupboard with paneled doors and single drawer below, c. 1830, refinished.

Pine and poplar 2-drawer jelly cupboard, bracket base and paneled doors, original un-
painted finish, found in eastern Virginia, c. 1870's.

Left:
Child's ladder-back chair, North Carolina, c. late 19th century.

Right:
Six-board blanket box with red comb graining and bun feet, Pennsylvania, c. 1840.
Painted dough box, c. mid 19th century. Late 19th century French carnival game.

Top:
Painted rope bed with elaborate headboard, c. 1840's. It is not a simple task to find a 19th century bed that is sturdy, maintains its original finish, and is not missing its rails. We recently purchased a low post maple and pine rope bed in North Carolina. It was in its original finish and had its rails, but it turned out to be less than sturdy. The bed was a great bed in all aspects but one. You could not sleep in it. Some antiques are decorative and others are decorative and functional. We thought we were buying a decorative bed that was also functional. We ended up spending more money to make the bed sturdy and sleepable. We bought somebody's problems and turned them into our problem.

Left:
Red painted cupboard, pine, c. 1870's.

Right:
Schoolmaster's desk, pine with lift lid, c. late 19th century.

Bottom:
Stack of boxes, mid to late 19th century. Butternut with three drawers, walnut with four drawers, pine with blue paint.

Left:
Open step-back cupboard, plate rails, North Carolina, c. 1860-1875,

Bottom:
Set of six half spindle-back chairs, factory made, c. 1860's-1870's.

Top:
Miniature blanket chest presented to Harrison Grant Horton by his grandfather in 1887, pine, found in North Carolina.

Bottom:
Decorated six-board blanket chest, bracket base, c. mid-19th century.

Left:

Refinished pie safe "star" tins, pine, c. 1860. Regardless of what you have been told, there is a wealth of pie safes available for your collection. A semi-trailer load could easily be arranged. There is one problem. The wealth of safes consists of pieces of furniture that have peeling paint, rusted tins, and some structural damage. We see pie safes almost everywhere we go that have been recently rescued from water-filled basements, abandoned barns, back porches, and collapsed houses. It is very difficult to locate a refinished safe similar to this example with decorative tins or a piece with its original paint in good shape.

Right:

Refinished pie safe with replaced screen wire inserts, factory made, c. 1900. A factory-made piece of furniture that has been "skinned" should have minimal value, but they turn up labeled as "country" each month in the home decorating magazines and thousands of hearts begin to flutter and prices rise.

Blue-grey "jelly" cupboard, original painted finish, c. mid 19th century.

Poplar and pine corner cupboard, c. 1850's.

Left:
Step-back "open" cupboard, original finish, c. 1880.

Right:
Pine and poplar cupboard, refinished, c. 1860.

Top:
Bracket base six-board blanket chest, strong blue paint, c. 1840.

Left:
Grain painted chimney cupboard, found in Kentucky, c. 1850.

Top:
Ten-foot settle bench, worn original finish, c. 1885.

Right:
Maple storage cupboard, mid-19th century, Kentucky.

Left:
Refinished pine step-back cupboard, c. 1850, filled with molded stoneware.

Right:
Pine hanging cupboard, paneled door, remnants of green paint, c. 1850.

Left:
Corner cupboard with painted grained exterior and
repainted interior, c. 1830.

Right:
Red pie cupboard, pine, North Carolina, c. 1860's.

Country Hepplewhite one-drawer drop leaf table, original red painted finish, c. 1830. Set of English bow-back Windsor chairs.

Left:
Pine pie safe, old red stain, bun feet, unusual gallery top with shelf, six hand-punched heart tins, c. 1860's, found in western Virginia.

Right:
Buttermolds and stamps, tin and walnut foot warmer with punched hearts and a wall of German springerle (cookie) molds.

Left:
Rare painted pine cupboard, step-back, Ohio, c. 1850's.

Bottom:
Bracket base six-board blanket box, early painted finish, c. 1840's.

Left:
Four-door blind front pine cupboard with traces of old paint, raised panel doors, found in Maine, c. 1870's.

Right:
Open step-back cupboard, pine with reddish-brown stain, found in Connecticut, late 19th century. Collection of redware pottery.

Top:
We have a special weakness for outdoor antiques markets filled with dealers who do not cart the same merchandise from show to show. The advantage of a one or two day outdoor show is that collectors rent space and bring pieces from their homes that may have been purchased 15 years before. The blue cupboard and hutch table were both fresh from collections and quickly sold.

Bottom:
High post rope bed, twin size, poplar, c. 1860's, red and white Lone Star quilt, double signed and dated "made by Lucinda Parker Walker 1835, quilted by Nettie Ripley 1937."

Late 18th century server, cherry, drawer and open shelf, scalloped gallery top.

Left:
Painted side or dining chair, white oak splint seat, North Carolina, c. late 19th century. The distance from the floor to the top of a chair seat should be approximately 16" to 18". Simple ladder-back country chairs similar to this example are not rare. In sets of four to six, they are much more difficult to find. All were painted originally and most had splint seats.

Bottom:
"Fancy" dining chairs with rush seats and newly stenciled decoration and paint, part of a set of six or eight chairs.

Top:
Pine gateleg dropleaf table, set of six lyre-back or fiddle-back chairs in mustard paint, mid-19th century.

Bottom:
Pine saw buck table with painted base and scrubbed top, late 19th century. Two spindle-back side or dining chairs, factory made, c. 1870's-1880's.

Top:
New England Pin Company display box from a variety store, c. 1900, original condition.

Left:
"Bird cage" Windsor arm chair, c. 1830's-1850, New England. The lack of wear on the seat of the chair spindles, and the general condition of the paint suggest that at some point in the not too distant past the chair has been repainted.

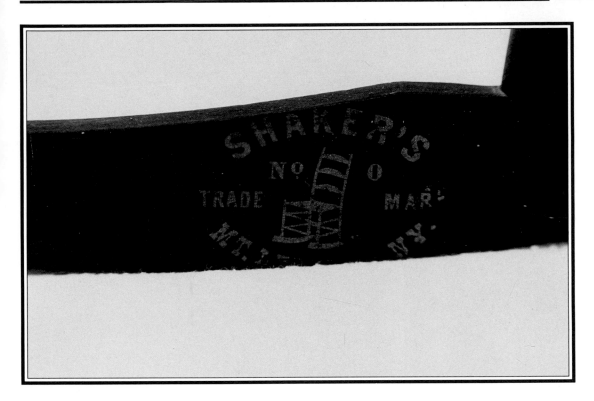

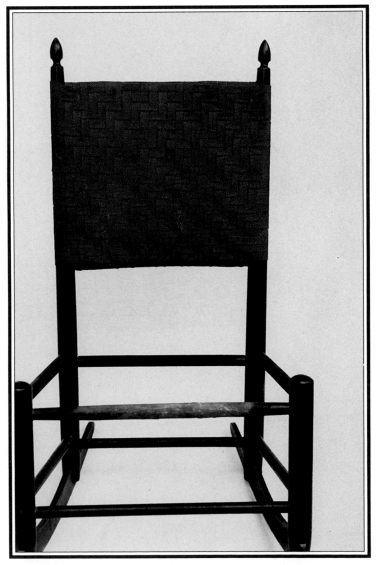

Top:
Shaker child's rocking chair, size zero, Mt. Lebanon, New York, ebony finish, c. 1900.

Right:
Shaker transfer or decal on inside of chair rocker. The transfers are seldom found on the chairs because they were easily washed off with soap and water.

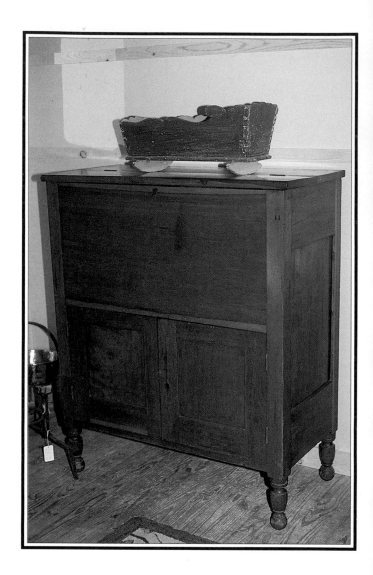

Left:
Refinished dry sink from the early 1900's.

Right:
Kentucky sugar chest, cherry, c. mid 19th century.

Left:
North Carolina pine "open" cupboard, white and green paint, c. 1870's.

Right:
"Glazed" front cupboard, pine, c. 1860, refinished.

Top:
Pine and maple plank seat settee, 6' long, c. late 19th century. Mid 19th century hooked rug found in Pennsylvania.

Left:
Bracket base cupboard, New England, c. 1840.

Top:

Shaker production ladder-back chair with a cushion rail, Mt. Lebanon, New York, late 19th century. Shaker bentwood rocking chair, taped seat and back, Mt. Lebanon, New York, c. 1880. The Shakers saw a bentwood rocking chair at the Philadelphia Exposition in 1876 and later offered their own version of the chair in their Mt. Lebanon catalogs. The chairs were not well received by customers at the time or by collectors today. A "production" chair is one made in quantity and offered for sale to the "world." "Community" chairs were usually specifically made for use by the Shaker brothers and sisters and used in their rooms or meeting houses.

Right:

Painted ladder-back rocking chair with "cheese cutter" rockers, bittersweet finish, New York state, c. mid 19th century, "acorn" finials. In many antiques shops this is a Shaker rocking chair because it has turned finials and a taped seat. It can best be described as "country" that originally had a splint seat that has been replaced with newly purchased woolen tapes.

Left:
Pine pie safe, painted finish, screen wire inserts, south eastern United States, c. 1880's.

Right:
Unusual pie cupboard, green paint, pierced tins, "boot jack" ends, original condition, c. 1860's-1870's.

Left:
Walnut six-board blanket chest with a bracket base, never painted, found in southeastern Virginia, c. 1850.

Bottom:
Pine dry sink, ochre paint, c. 1880.

Left:
Pie safe with tin pierced "star" tins and turned legs, Kentucky, c. 1870.

Right:
Two-piece painted step-back cupboard, replaced pulls, c. 1880, Ohio.

Top:
Six-board blanket chest, late paint, c. 1880-1900.

Bottom:
Blue-green lamp or bedside table, tapered pine legs, probability of replaced top, c. 1860.

Top:

Six-board blanket chest with turned feet, lift lid, paint of indeterminate age. The paint on this blanket chest was not hand-carried in a pail on the Mayflower. It might have been delivered in a pail by Federal Express or hand-carried to the parking lot at the local K Mart.

Bottom:

In the 1920's, *Antiques Magazine* usually carried an ad for repainted 50-year-old blanket chests that could be used in homes attempting to secure the "colonial" look. The pieces were painted to resemble Pennsylvania dower chests. The paint on these chests is now three generations old. They have been exposed to children, light, dust, and periodic use. Keep in mind that the chests date from the 1840-1870 period and with worn, 70-year-old paint are going to fool a lot of people.

Left:
Pine cupboard with paneled doors, c. 1880. Six-board blanket chest in dark blue paint, pine, c. 1860-1880.

Right:
Late 19th century pine cupboard, step-back, refinished.

Left:
Refinished pine step-back, "open" cupboard, collection of butter prints and molds.

Right:
Late 19th century chest of drawers, original finish, factory made.

Oak grained pine cupboard, possibly an architectural or built-in piece, c. 1850's-1870's.

Maple and pine pie safe, screen wire inserts, c. 1900, never painted.

North Carolina pine cupboard, "boot jact" ends, probably designed to fit in between two walls because the sides are not painted, c. 1890-early 1900's.

Blind front pine cupboard, raised panel doors, original blue-grey paint, found in West Virginia. Stack of painted boxes.

Left:
Painted table, factory made, maple and pine, c. 1900.

Bottom:
Sycamore meat block, turned legs, early 1900's.

Right:
Green sponge decorated storage box, New England, c. 1830's. Pine factory-made trunk, refinished, c. 1900.

Bottom:
Pine dome top trunk with worn green paint, c. 1840's. Dovetailed blanket chest, red "wash," c. 1860. A "wash" is a mixture of water and paint that allows the grain of the wood to show through.

Left:
Hanging shelves with collections of treen (wooden) barrels and banks, wooden toy tops, and kitchen tinware.

Bottom:
Walnut plantation desk from Kentucky with "glazed" upper section, c. 1850.

Painted pine cupboard, North Carolina, c. 1860's.

Rare three-door pine cupboard, original apple green paint, c. 1870's, probably had wooden drawer pulls rather than porcelain.

Top:
Bracket-base blanket chest, c. 1860's.

Right:
"As found" pie safe, pine, painted finish, "star" tins, c. 1870's-1880's.

Left:
Painted wash stand with wooden bowl, Illinois, early 1900's.

Right:
Oak grained blanket chest, paneled sides, c. 1880.

Right:
Painted storage cupboard, c. late 19th century.

Bottom:
Refinished pine cupboard, c. early 1900's.

Right:
Great blue drysink, New York state, c. 1870.

Bottom:
Painted low-post rope bed, c. mid 19th century.

North Carolina hunt board, c. 1850.

Pennsylvania bucket bench, original red paint, c. 1860's.

Top:
Mt. Lebanon, New York, Shaker rocking chair, replaced woolen tapes, c. 1880.

Right:
Kentucky cupboard, poplar and walnut, c. 1850's.

Top:
Blue sugar chest with drawer, pine, turned legs, c. 1840's-1850's.

Left:
Blue-grey pine cupboard, paneled doors, c. mid 19th century.

Storage cupboard designed to be placed under a staircase, slanted top, c. 1860's.

Top:
Ladder-back country side chairs, two with white oak splint seats, c. late 19th century.

Left:
Grey cupboard from Pennsylvania or New York state, c. 1870's. This cupboard could be taken directly from the field where it was offered for sale and put in your home. The paint is "right" and it is a functional and attractive piece of furniture.

Left:

The dramatic increase in prices at auction for exceptional pieces of decorated salt glazed stoneware is largely due to the growing demand for American folk art. Elaborate scenes like this example on stoneware are extremely rare. This New York state piece dates from the 1870's. A piece of this quality can be cracked or chipped and still have significant value.

Right:

Eight-gallon Greensboro, Pennsylvania, stoneware jar, decorated by stencil and brush, c. 1880's.

Left:
Great stenciled American eagle on Pennsylvania jar, combination of brushed and stenciled decoration is uncommon, c. 1880's.

Right:
Two-gallon jar and three-gallon butter churn, brushed capacity marks, mid 19th century.

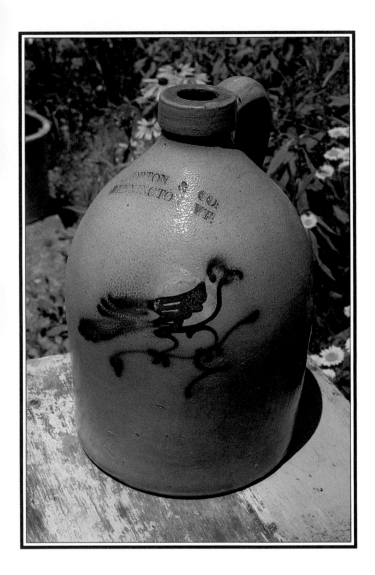 

Left:
Bennington, Vermont "bird" jar. In 1969, this jug could have been purchased for $40.00-50.00 in many antiques shops in New York state and New England.

Right:
Two-gallon jug, slip trailed decoration of a flower, probably sold as a "second" at the pottery, c. 1870's-1880's.

Left:

Four-gallon unmarked crock, probably midwestern, c. 1880's, inverted Christmas tree decoration done with a slip-cup. The stoneware business had become so competitive and mechanical by the 1880's that pieces were rarely decorated to any extent. Occasionally a piece would be specially ordered and decorated as a gift or presentation award. This crock was decorated in seconds and moved on down the line. If a piece of this quality has semi-serious cracks or chips, it is almost without value.

Right:

Buffalo, New York, jug with cobalt initials, ovoid form, c. early 1840's. An ovoid or pear-shaped jug has broad shoulders that taper to a smaller base. This classic form began to change in the early 1840's and by the 1880's, churns, jugs, crocks, and jars had cylindrical sides. The ovoids took more talent to make and were more susceptible to breakage while being transported.

Left:
Brushed cobalt decoration on 1860's crock filled with fresh flowers.

Right:
Collection of stoneware canning jars.

Left:
J. Norton and Co., Bennington, Vermont, "bird" jar
with impressed maker's and capacity marks.

Right:
Cobalt decorated jugs, c. 1840's-1880.

Right:
Molded utilitarian stoneware was produced in huge quantities from the 1880's well into the 20th century. With the exception of a pitcher and decorated crock on the upper shelf, all of the stoneware in the cupboard were molded rather than individually thrown on a potter's wheel.

Bottom left:
Dated pieces of stoneware are not commonly found. This "1892" example was thrown on a potter's wheel. Compare its cylindrical sides to the earlier ovoid pieces.

Bottom right:
This "1865" piece was also "thrown" rather than molded. Note changes in form between the "1865" piece and the "1892."

Collection of molded yellow ware, c. 1880-1920.

Left:
A striking variety of molded and thrown stoneware bottles, jugs, and pitchers.

Right:
Molded stoneware mixing bowls, c. early 1900's.

Top:
Brush decorated stoneware bowls, "thrown," c. 1860's-1880.

Left:
Five-gallon Macomb, Illinois butter churn, replaced wooden dasher and lid, c. 20th century, stenciled pottery and capacity mark.

Left:
Three-gallon molded Macomb crock, Bristol (white) glaze, stenciled, 20th century.

Right:
Collection of graniteware and molded stoneware, 20th century.

Left:
The distinction between a reproduction and a fake is important. Potter Jerry Beaumont (pictured with his father) creates reproduction stoneware in his York, Maine, kiln. A reproduction is designed to capture the spirit of an original piece. It is not made to deceive or entice someone to pay a great deal of money for something they are not receiving. Beaumont's stoneware has original designs completed with a slip-cup or brush. Each piece has the maker's mark impressed into the clay and a signature or initials and date incised into its bottom. As is the case with many pieces of quality contemporary folk art, much of Beaumont's work has increased in value over the years.

Bottom:
Four Beaumont crocks and a "bird" jar.

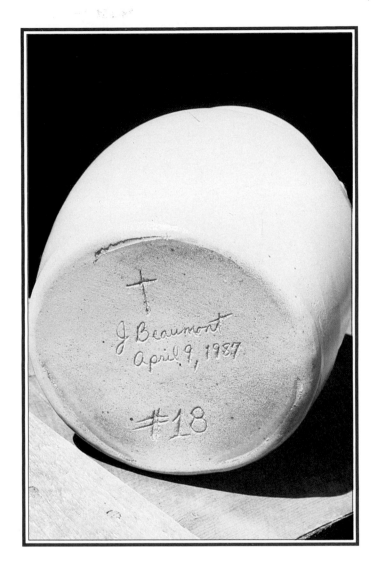

Left:
Slip-trailed limited edition stoneware jar.

Right:
Incised signature and date on bottom of jar.

Left:
If this decorated stoneware bird bath was old, you would have to sell several rooms of your house and an uncle to buy it. The basket of flowers decoration was done with a slip-cup.

Right:
The illusion is spoiled a bit when you see more than one.

Contemporary salt glazed miniature stoneware made to one-twelfth scale by the Vernon Pottery of Virginia Beach, Virginia.

Left:
Contemporary "grotesque" redware jug with double handles.

Bottom:
Ovoid jug, no maker's mark or decoration, classic "pear-shaped" form.

Contemporary pottery decorated with a slip cup from the Bon Aqua, Tennessee Pottery.

Top:
Painted splint utility basket. Baskets are extremely difficult to date. Handcrafted baskets have been made in much the same way for more than a century. Daily use and exposure to dirt, sunlight, and the weather can make a two-year-old basket appear to be an "antique." An "antique" basket can be 100-years-old or 30-years-old if its purpose for being made was utilitarian. Painted baskets are much more difficult to obtain. This is at least a $200.00 basket. The basket is worth about $75.00 and it has a $125.00 coat of old red paint.

Left:
Splint gathering basket, white oak. If the paint on this basket is old, it is a significant piece of American folk art. It may be a piece of folk art but the paint is not old. Country baskets were functional. They were designed to be used. This example gives no evidence of wear or use.

Left:

Painted basket used to carry small logs or pieces of kindling. Due to the way it was used, we would expect the paint to exhibit considerable wear. The handle should be worn to a much greater degree.

Right:

Tobacco drying basket, Kentucky, machine cut splint, nailed together, early 20th century. On the West Coast, these baskets could be priced at more than $100.00 each. In Kentucky, Virginia, Tennessee, and the Carolinas, there are still warehouses and drying barns filled with them at a considerably discounted rate.

Top:
Melon basket, oak splint.

Bottom:
Collection of country baskets. The round basket with the open weave bottom was used to separate curds and whey. The basket was put over a crock and a piece of cheese cloth was put in the basket. The mixture was poured through the cloth and the cheese curds stayed in the basket. The whey was fed to the hogs. Cheese baskets are rarely found today.

Top:
Melon basket and bushel basket, oak splint.

Bottom:
Variety of ash and oak splint baskets.

Left:
Painted feather storage basket with lid, early 20th century.

Bottom:
"Buttocks" basket, used for gathering eggs or garden produce, "as found" condition. The buttocks form allowed the contents of the basket to be evenly distributed on both sides and not fall through the center.

Top:
Oak splint utility baskets and a refinished six-board blanket chest, c. 1850.

Bottom:
Handcrafted basket makers found the market for their product almost gone after 1890. At that point a machine was in general use that cut splint in huge quantities at a minimal cost. Basket making before 1890 was highly labor-intensive. Individuals, families, and even small villages in rural areas made baskets for sale to the surrounding area one at a time. They could not compete with mass-produced baskets and most went out of business.

Utility basket, oak splint, "as found" condition.

Top:
Splint market basket, hand crafted, white oak.

Bottom:
Rare woven child's cradle made from oak splint, pine rockers, late 19th century.

Capital coffee bin, c. 1900-1915.

Right:
Coffee grinder, original painted finish, replaced drawer, c. 1910.

Bottom:
Metal flag holder, c. 1915.

Left:
Metal "Pepsi" menu board, c.1950.

Right:
The regional influence on antiques and collectibles is always interesting. We have seen more unusual Coca-Cola machines for sale in North Carolina than anywhere else in America.

Top:
1950's Coca-Cola machine.

Bottom:
Zinc-lined Whistle soft drink box, slide top, possibly used in a gas station or small grocery store, c. 1940's.

Brown's Seeds display counter for seed packets, c. 1920. Collectors who search diligently for items that decorated the counters and shelves of grocery stores between the 1880's and 1920 are very concerned about the condition of the items they purchase. If the items have been repainted or repaired, most country store collectors have no interest. For the past 15 years we have collected seed boxes with colorful interior and exterior labels. We were foolish enough to write an article for a popular country magazine extolling the virtues of seed boxes. We quickly found that many of the readers of the magazine had suddenly decided that seed boxes were highly collectible and prices soared.

The five photos that follow are from a collection in Nashville, Tennessee.

Wooden washing machine, factory made, painted blue, c. 1910.

Left:
Painted pine box used to store shoe shine supplies, found in North Carolina, c. 1930.

Bottom:
Painted cast iron andirons, c. 19th century.

Left:
Sunday School register, c. early 1900's.

Right:
Cast iron hitching post, original painted finish, c. 1850.

Bisque-head doll purchased in 1913 at Fisher's Department Store in Dupo, Illinois. The doll has porcelain teeth, human hair, and pierced ears.

Top:
Blue knife and fork box, splayed sides, c. early 1900's.

Bottom:
Carpenter's tool box, painted pine, c. early 1900's.

Left:
Chalk cat, possibly a carnival booth prize, c. 1930's-1940's.

Bottom:
Painted American eagle, cast zinc, repainted, c. 1880-1920.

Top:
Unusual painted instrument or tool case, dome top, c. 1900.

Bottom:
Wagon wheel, c. early 1900's.

Homemade game or checker boards are very collectible. Numerous magazine articles and several books have been written about the boards. The majority date from the 1870-1920 period and are usually nailed together from pine or poplar. Typically the more colorfully a board is painted, the more difficult it is to find and the higher the price tag. The underside of a board usually is not painted and may carry running scores from games played generations ago. Initials and a carved date occasionally are found. If the board has been painted on its underside, the paint should be scratched and worn in places from being moved around the table.

As is the case with many of the pieces illustrated in this book, there are numerous contemporary artists who design and make reproductions and others who attempt to profit from fakes. An "old" game board should show wear on its painted surface because checkers were not picked up and placed on a square, they were pushed. Scratches, time, spills, cigar ashes, and an upset loser who kicked the board to the floor all take their toll.

Game boards can show up almost anywhere because they were in use well into the 20th century. With the growing popularity of mass-produced and heavily advertised board games after World War I, many game boards were put in the attic or the bottom of a closet.

The game boards that follow all date from the late 19th century to about 1920.

Left:
Staved yellow bucket with metal bands, c. early 1900's.

Stack of painted measures and covered boxes, c. late 19th century.

Blue painted barrel, staved, metal bands, c. early 1900's.

Three painted sugar buckets, factory made, staved construction with "drop" handles, c. early 20th century. Sugar buckets and pantry boxes were rarely "signed" or marked by the factory in which they were made. They are found in a variety of sizes with the large and small buckets and boxes the most difficult to find.

Left:

Painted pantry boxes, c. late 19th century. Pantry boxes were mass-produced in woodenware factories from the 1870's until well into the 20th century. The value of a pantry box is determined by its condition and the color of its painted finish.

Right:

The collector of kitchen and hearth antiques must keep an especially watchful eye out for imports. Spain, Mexico, and Portugal have provided many "early American" antiques to shops. The mortars and pestles on the second shelf are representative of many that have been imported in quantity.

Top:
Factory-made Noah's ark, c. early 20th century.

Right:
A wall of late 19th - early 20th century "smalls."

Painted wagons or wheelbarrows that are 50 to 75 years old are difficult to locate in reasonably good repair. Like many country antiques they were functional and not ornamental. They were used until they were broken to the point they could not be fixed. Most homemade wheelbarrows are impossible to accurately date because they may be constructed of bits and pieces of three or four other wheelbarrows that were left for parts. The four wheelbarrows pictured here appear to be in their original condition and date from the early 1900's to approximately 1940.

A century old wheelbarrow or birdhouse would be a major rarity. Most birdhouse that are offered for sale at shows and markets and in shops date from the 1930's to the 1960's. Many collectors paid little attention to birdhouses until a profusely illustrated article or two appeared in the major "country decorating" magazines. After the articles many collectors believed that birdhouses were significant pieces of American folk art and began to knock on doors and attempt to make purchases out of backyard trees.

The three birdhouses that are pictured date from the 1930's to the 1950's.

Bottom:

About 20 years ago, we visited a small village that specialized in antiques shops. One of the shops was operated by a nationally-known dealer in American antiques. He had a pile of wooden bowls in the shop that went from the floor to the ceiling. When we inquired about the source of so many bowls, he said that he had purchased a collection of them that had been stored in a barn for many years. An examination of the bowls found that many were repaired with lids from tin cans. The writing on the lids was difficult to read. The difficulty was not in the condition of the lids, but in the language on them. It was Spanish.

Whenever you see stacks of anything "old," a red flag should appear and engulf your checkbook before you can get it out. This stack of wooden bowls is overpriced and underdated and could have some can lids in Spanish attached.

Top:
Collection of home spun, 19th century.

Left:
Ohio coverlet from the 1840's and midwestern quilts from the 1920's and 1930's.

Top:
Child's factory-made rocking horse, c. 1940.

Right:
Painted metal watering can, c. 1900. Staved green bucket with lid, c. 1870.

Left:
Dasher wooden butter churn, original lid with handle, metal bands, c. 1860-1870.

Bottom:
Collection of cast iron regulator and windmill weights, c. 1900.

Top:
Fairbury, Nebraska cast iron bull, c. early 1900's.

Bottom:
Rare painted buffalo windmill weight, c. 1900.

Left:
Cast iron counter balance weight from an early 1900's windmill.

Right:
Cast iron Eclipse weights, c. 1915.

Boss bull and Dempster horse weights, cast iron, c. 1910.

Top:
Painted pine box with slide lid, found in Kentucky, c. 1850.

Left:
Unusual painted shelves, pine, c. late 19th century.

Contemporary coverlet woven to order by Red Lion, Pennsylvania artisian David Kline.

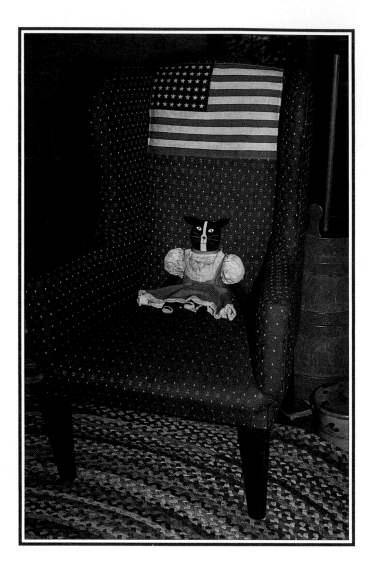

Left:
You can spend thousands on an old chair frame and have it covered with new fabric or several hundred on a new chair with the same fabric and be able to sit on it. The purist who wants everything from "the period" tends to lose his lunch when checks are written for 18th century wing chairs.

Right:
Game board painted by artist Mary Myers of Virginia Beach, Virginia.

Maryland carver Jack Hughes is one of the nation's premier carver of decoys.

Left:
Intricately-made windmill with a clock mechanism, dates from the early 20th century and was found in Kentucky.

Right:
Bridal couple carved by Sharon Pierce.

These sculptured rag dolls are made and dressed by Jan Farley of Blue Grass, Iowa.

Collectible cardboard or pressed paper Easter rabbits that were sold filled with candy in the 1930's until well into the 1950's.

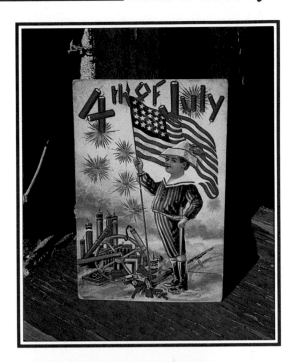

In recent years there have been several shows that only feature dealers with Christmas, Halloween, and other holiday antiques and collectibles. Items range from Christmas ornaments and cardboard pumpkins to a variety of holiday postcards that date from the 1880's to 1930.

"Feather" Christmas trees were imported from Germany and Austria from the 1890's until the 1930's. The trees were sold in sizes ranging from 10 inches to 7 feet.

Top left:

Boxes of Christmas decorations can turn up at almost any garage or tag sale because everyone had a tree and a door to hang things on. This glass ornament was found at a rural Illinois auction for a few dollars. It dates from about 1920.

Top right, bottom left:

Contemporary Christmas ornaments made by Twins Feather Trees of Cincinnati, Ohio.

Bottom right:

Santa's stocking was made by Suzanne Kennedy of Rochester, New York and the box dates from the 1930's.

Top left:
Pressed paper "trick or treat" pumpkin, c. 1950.

Top right:
Mass-produced pumpkins from the 1950's.

Left:
Metal candy container, c. 1940's.

Price Guide
to

Book of Country

Volume II

Price Guide

No values are listed for contemporary country items.

Page 9
Refinished step-back cupboard $1000.00-1200.00
Pine table $800.00-1000.00

Page 10
Corner cupboard $1300.00-1600.00
Pine blanket chest $450.00-550.00

Page 11
Dome top box $140.00-160.00
"Jelly" cupboard $1500.00-1700.00

Page 12
Child's chair $50.00-75.00
Hepplewhite chest $1800.00-2000.00

Page 13
Trestle table $1750.00-2000.00
Storage chest $450.00-550.00

Page 14
24-drawer chest $750.00-1000.00
Pine cupboard $1700.00-2400.00

Page 15
Apothecary chest $1500.00-2000.00
Federal chest $1200.00-1400.00

Page 16
Pine cupboard $400.00-500.00
Rocking chair $150.00-185.00

Page 17
Green farm table $550.00-625.00

Page 18
Storage cupboard $950.00-1100.00

Page 19
Rocking chair $325.00-375.00
Bedside table $50.00-75.00

Page 20
Windsor chair $1800.00-2200.00
Painted cupboard $800.00-975.00

Page 21
Pine pie cupboard $600.00-700.00

Page 22
Open cupboard $700.00-900.00

Page 23
"Barrel front" cupboard $1450.00-1500.00
Painted pine cupboard $800.00-900.00

Page 24
Sugar chest $2200.00-2600.00

Page 25
Cupboard $650.00-800.00
Paneled door cupboard $750.00-1000.00

Page 26
Pine and poplar cupboard $700.00-800.00

Page 27
Child's chair $50.00-75.00
Blanket box $700.00-785.00

Page 28
Rope bed $800.00-900.00
Red cupboard $550.00-650.00

Page 29
Schoolmaster's desk $400.00-500.00
Boxes .... each $200.00-300.00
Bed $750.00-850.00

Page 30
Cupboard $600.00-750.00
Set of chairs $1800.00-2200.00

Page 31
Bittersweet miniature chest $400.00-500.00
Decorated chest $600.00-750.00

Page 32
Refinished pie safe $450.00-550.00
Pie safe $500.00-575.00

Page 62
Grained cupboard $2800.00-3000.00

Page 63
Pie safe $500.00-600.00

Page 64
North Carolina cupboard $500.00-600.00

Page 65
Painted cupboard $2500.00-3000.00

Page 66
Painted table $200.00-250.00
Meat block....................................$300.00-400.00

Page 67
Green trunk $450.00-525.00
Dome top trunk $500.00-685.00

Page 68
Shelves..$550.00-650.00
Plantation desk........................$3000.00-3500.00

Page 69
Painted cupboard $1700.00-2000.00

Page 70
Rare three-door cupboard $3000.00-3500.00

Page 71
Blanket chest $375.00-450.00
Pie safe $400.00-450.00

Page 72
Painted wash stand.....................$500.00-575.00
Oak grained chest $400.00-450.00

Page 73
Storage cupboard $675.00-750.00
Refinished cupboard $750.00-800.00

Page 74
Blue sink $1200.00-1400.00
Low-post bed $600.00-650.00

Page 75
Hunt board $700.00-800.00

Page 76
Bucket bench $775.00-875.00

Page 77
Shaker rocking chair.................$800.00-1000.00
Kentucky cupboard $575.00-700.00

Page 78
Blue sugar chest $1300.00-1500.00
Pine cupboard $900.00-1000.00

Page 79
Storage cupboard $1200.00-1400.00

Page 80
Ladder-back side chairs ....each $50.00-75.00
Grey cupboard..............................$650.00-750.00

Page 81
Stoneware jar $475.00-600.00

Page 82
Eagle jar $1200.00-1400.00
Three-gallon churn $275.00-350.00

Page 83
"Bird" jug.....................................$385.00-450.00
Two-gallon jug $200.00-285.00

Page 84
Four-gallon crock $100.00-125.00
Initialed jug $150.00-175.00

Page 85
Canning jars ....each $55.00-200.00

Page 86
J. Norton jar $650.00-750.00
Cobalt jugs ....each $150.00-400.00

Page 87
"1892" jug $165.00-200.00
"1865" jug $175.00-225.00

Page 90
Brush-decorated bowls ....each $225.00-275.00
Five-gallon churn $150.00-175.00

Page 91
Three-gallon crock $75.00-100.00

Page 96
Basket...$175.00-200.00

Page 98
Utility basket $200.00-225.00

Page 99
Kindling basket $50.00-75.00
Tobacco basket...............................$75.00-100.00

Page 100
Melon basket $140.00-160.00

Page 101
Bushel basket............................$200.00-225.00
Churn $275.00-325.00

Page 102
Feather basket............................$150.00-200.00
Buttocks basket $135.00-185.00

Page 103
Blanket chest $200.00-250.00

Page 104
Utility basket...................................$25.00-35.00

Page 105
Market basket $100.00-125.00
Cradle $500.00-600.00

Page 106
Baskets ....each $75.00-150.00
Cheese basket $600.00-675.00

Page 107
Bin..$600.00-750.00
Coffee bin $400.00-500.00

Page 108
Coffee bin $350.00-400.00

Page 109
Coffee grinder $425.00-500.00
Flag holder $45.00-75.00

Page 110
Menu board......................................$25.00-30.00
Coke® machine $200.00-300.00

Page 111
Coke® machine $400.00-475.00
Whistle box..................................$250.00-300.00

Page 112
Brown's seed cabinet
  ....(cabinet only) $375.00-400.00

Page 115
Washing machine $225.00-275.00

Page 116
Shoe shine box $100.00-135.00
Cast iron andirons $250.00-300.00

Page 117
Register $100.00-150.00
Hitching post $2500.00-3500.00

Page 118
Stools ....each $55.00-75.00

Page 119
Quilt $325.00-450.00
Yarn winder $125.00-140.00

Page 121
Knife and fork box......................$140.00-160.00
Carpenter's box $75.00-100.00

Page 122
Chalk cat.......................................$50.00-75.00
Eagle $2000.00-2500.00

Page 128
Blue barrel $250.00-300.00

Page 129
Sugar bucket ....each $200.00-250.00

Page 130
Painted pantry boxes ....each $175.00-200.00

Page 132
Wheelbarrows........................each $225.00-300.00

Page 133
Wheelbarrows........................each $225.00-300.00

Page 134
Bird houses ....each $100.00-150.00

Page 135
Bird house...................................$100.00-125.00
Wooden bowls..........................each $35.00-50.00

Page 137
Rocking horse.............................$125.00-150.00
Watering can $55.00-65.00

Page 138
Dasher churn $275.00-350.00
Weights ....each $150.00-400.00

Page 139
Bull...$600.00-700.00
Buffalo $1200.00-1600.00

Page 140
Eclipse weights ....each $145.00-160.00

Page 141
Bull...$600.00-700.00
Horse $350.00-400.00

Page 142
Pine box $85.00-95.00

Page 146
Windmill $375.00-500.00

Page 148
Rabbits ....each $35.00-65.00

Page 149
Cards ....each $15.00-20.00

Page 150
Feather trees ....each $500.00-1000.00

Page 152
Pumpkin $85.00-100.00
Metal pumpkins ....each $65.00-75.00

Other Books by the Raycrafts

Collector's Guide to Country Stoneware & Pottery $9.95
Book of Country, Volume I...$19.95
Collector's Guide to Country Furniture, Book I..................$9.95
Collector's Guide to Country Furniture, Book II...............$14.95
Collector's Guide to Country Store Antiques....................$19.95
Collector's Guide to Country Baskets $9.95

All the above titles may be ordered from:

Collector Books
P.O. Box 3009
Paducah, Kentucky   42001

Add $2.00 for postage and handling.

Schroeder's Antiques Price Guide

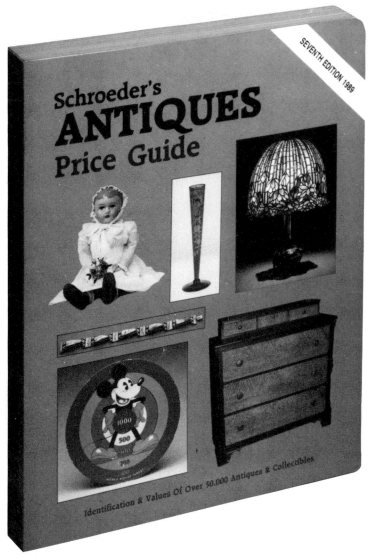

Schroeder's Antiques Price Guide has climbed its way to the top in a field already supplied with several well-established publications! The word is out, *Schroeder's Price Guide* is the best buy at any price. Over 500 categories are covered, with more than 50,000 listings. But it's not volume alone that makes Schroeder's the unique guide it is recognized to be. From ABC Plates to Zsolnay, if it merits the interest of today's collector, you'll find it in Schroeder's. Each subject is represented with histories and background information. In addition, hundreds of sharp original photos are used each year to illustrate not only the rare and the unusual, but the everyday "fun-type" collectibles as well -- not postage stamp pictures, but large close-up shots that show important details clearly.

Each edition is completely re-typeset from all new sources. We have not and will not simply change prices in each new edition. All new copy and all new illustrations make Schroeder's THE price guide on antiques and collectibles.

The writing and researching team behind this giant is proportionately large. It is backed by a staff of more than seventy of Collector Books' finest authors, as well as a board of advisors made up of well-known antique authorities and the country's top dealers, all specialists in their fields. Accuracy is their primary aim. Prices are gathered over the entire year previous to publication, from ads and personal contacts. Then each category is thoroughly checked to spot inconsistencies, listings that may not be entirely reflective of actual market dealings, and lines too vague to be of merit. Only the best of the lot remains for publication. You'll find *Schroeder's Antiques Price Guide* the one to buy for factual information and quality.

No dealer, collector or investor can afford not to own this book. It is available from your favorite bookseller or antiques dealer at the low price of $12.95. If you are unable to find this price guide in your area, it's available from Collector Books, P. O. Box 3009, Paducah, KY 42001 at $12.95 plus $2.00 for postage and handling.

8½ x 11, 608 Pages $12.95

COLLECTOR BOOKS
A Division of Schroeder Publishing Co., Inc.